Lyric

First published in April 2016 by Zest Press, an Imprint of Fair Acre Press

Published with the generous support of
BirTh the Birmingham Transmedia Research Hub,
The School of Visual Communications Birmingham City University
and Wenlock Poetry Festival

ISBN 978-10911048-19-0

Printed by Azimuth Print Ltd
Unit 2A, Princess Street, Bedminster, Bristol BS3 4AG
https://www.azimuthprint.co.uk

"Orpheus' lute was strung with poets' sinews"

The Two Gentlemen of Verona, 3.2.79

Songwriting. Songwrighting. Songrighting. It's alchemikal. It's a weaving of word and tone as warp and weft, a melding of base material in pursuit of something precious – stirring egg yolk and ochre in a boiling crucible, hoping for gold. It's like Frankenstein or Franklin grounding lightning to some purpose, or the universal clockmaker, fiddling by candlelight. It's a short fat Coleridge with a belly ache humming to the mists at Grasmere. It's writing as a poet, a novelist or a diarist, wrighting like a machinist or a coder or a mechanic, righting like a prophet or a priest or politician.

Lately I've come across poets and poetry thinkers who have divorced us. Thrown the songwriter out of the word–workers party, for a number of reasons. Songs are unpredictable, says one – we listen rather than look, so that the essential circumscription of a poem on a page is lost to a song, whose ending may be intuited from its form but never perfectly predicted until it's enacted. Another sees the whiteness of the page eating the songwriters' words the moment they are orphaned from the when-shall-we-three meet-again of melody, harmony and rhythm. This one continues with a request that no one ever talk to him again about songs and poetry. An unhappy divorce for him, it would seem, with wounds that still run deep.

I think I understand. Like Keats so many of us eschew the alarum of popular praise, saying with him that our works are for the discerning – or maybe not even for other human ears at all, in some cases. Fame may, as songwriter Nick Drake says, be "but a fruit tree, so very unsound", but songwriters – or some of them at least - are feted and rewarded, celebrated, applauded and their pockets stuffed with money until they're bloated and rich as Croesus. Never in my life have I seen the same for a poet. Take the recent beatification of Bowie, a words and melody man widely hailed as more humanly significant than Popes, Actors or Emperors – and by extension than poets.

Oh but wait a minute, slowly now, I seem to be saying this separation of lyricist and poet is real, that one is fish and one is foul – that is not what I am about. So here it is, my thesis: poetry and songwriting are more the same than they are different. The problem for those 'pro-poetry' divisionist writers I've cited above is the page, and the illusion it has spun that the home of poetry is there. I love the page too. I like textured paper the most. Something that my fingers feel as they wander in the whiteness, an undiscovered country, an image of the transcendent, the featureless but fecund and incalculably beautiful place beyond the white gate, described so

perfectly in Zen. A place I want to dwell in and linger, the place from which I draw strength, which makes the drudgery and boredom of the everyday bearable, knowing I will be back there at some point, soon or late. When I was a child Ted Hughes showed it to me in his *Thought Fox* – the midnight outside, the empty page before the poet, until with the "short sharp stink of fox" the page was printed, the poem incarnated. The making of the poem, which leads us always back to the potential of the page. But is that where poetry lives, those black ciphers on white? These letters which I'm writing and you're reading are nothing more than conventions, squiggles that symbolise sounds that (with geographical, cultural and temporal limits) are associated with fragments of meaning. They are socially mediated and malleable, always in the process of negotiation and collapse, so that at a little distance or across a surprisingly short time the squiggles mean nothing to most people and the sounds are indecipherable. Can these codes really embody, really be poetry? Chinese writing is entirely other. Instead of marks that represent sound, their strokes of colour on a ground directly incite meaning (well mostly anyway). So a poem written in Chinese characters can be read in Putong Hwa, or Guangdong Hwa, or Hokkien, sounding differently but meaning the same. Even so we see both eastern and western poetry as essentially similar, ignoring the double symbolic system of the west, against the single of the east – acting as if you can translate the multi dimensionality of pictographic writing so long as you roughly know the 'meaning'. It seems then that the nature and character of the signification is subordinate to the 'something' that the symbols on paper represent. And it is between the signification and the 'something' that 'being poetry' lies.

What then is the something? If Chinese poetry works with entirely different sounds in different spoken languages can it really be just about words? I would be foolish in one way to say it's not. Poetry is so often and so much about word play, specific to its place, time and community, celebrating the particular and time limited iteration of the human voice and mind playing with sound. In pictographic languages, though, poetry exceeds sound and so exists directly in the tension and articulation between representative image and meaning. In phonetically written languages, writing directly represents sounds, so that poetry must exist in the tension between meaning and sound.

The sound of the phonemes as they flow, the resonance in the skull, the rattling of our bones. Transmission in the braincase, electrical flow between cochlea, inner ear and grey matter, the buzzing of our teeth as we speak. The grounding and shorting of the manipulated groans and squeaks and grunts, so that all the clicks and warbles of our sound creating possibilities become attached to dreams and imaginations, descriptions and intuitions. I love the black on white of a poem on a page, but it is a repository, an arcane and beautiful extension of the profound promethean moment when we speak. In defence of song I need to argue that the poetic moment, the poetic heart lies not on the page: the black on white is in service to the word sounded in the mind, and, further, the net of implications and intuitions that those imagined phonemes carry/signify.

I'm coming to a close now, in case you're losing patience. Homer's Odyssey and Iliad were so beautifully sung (he is called almost always the singer) by this illiterate wonder that someone thought to write down the words. And Shakespeare. Is there a greater poet? And it is he that we are celebrating above all others at this festival. Did he write the plays? Scribbling in an attic like Joseph Fiennes in *Shakespeare in Love*? Or more like his own self emanation perhaps, Prospero in *The Tempest*, shaking then breaking the staff of his power, summoning spirits of the air to his bidding before, decrepit, finally letting them go. No one knows if he with pen himself wrote the plays, or if some other, listening to the spoken words on stage, copied them down in a dubious deed of plagiarism and piracy for which so many us are eternally grateful. Not writing then, but speaking. And singing.

Finally to Theodore Adorno – and an admission. He is a philosopher who thinks that popular music is reductive, always using the same very limited harmonic structures and predictable melodies. He is both right and wrong. So much of this music is exactly as he describes, fulfilling in its comforting predictability a social need for reassurance in this wild and strange Universe. Music functioning like concrete and street lighting, divorcing and shielding tiny, timid humanity from the immensity of its context. But so much of 'pop' music is entirely other – pushing the limits and boundaries of who we are, picking at the holes of our hermetic, socially–mediated world views and waking the imaginations of generations. I have represented both poles in this short collection, and touch moments in all the territories between. I don't want to pull any punches or tell it like it isn't. Look for the pages where the white eats the words and those where it does not. I have my view, and I am interested in yours. I have enjoyed the conversation so far, and I hope you will too.

Jonathan **Day**
Penybontfawr March 2016

Andrew Kulman.

The Rehearsal (for Elizabeth Bishop)

Today I saw a Pelican bowing the ocean,
elbowed and flailing for a pick at the fill,
and the blue of a flame was the blue of the ocean,
all of the rest that you could fit in a bill,

And up on the desk was an island of papers,
a volume of Lowell and a clutch of your letters.

So maybe I'll put the French Horn in a letter,
tell about the Pelican, tell about the Flame,
walk to the water with my fist in a fetter,
tied around an envelope burying your name,

and maybe these old velum gulls will take wing,
the boats in the quay or the sun in the evening.

Oh I spent a year at the maw of a sonnet,
with a woman so tender at the fore of the fray,
the glory of Rome was a bow in her bonnet,
and all of the rest they never built in a day,

and her hair was the hue of the water I knew,
the dark of a kiss and of faces at mourning.

I knew a house, all clapboard and wicker,
down the years to a door,
and these things we forefend,
and if I'd have known how, I'd have gotten there quicker,
but I didn't know how.

Today I saw a pelican bowing the ocean
elbowed and flailing for a pick at the fill,
and the blue of a flame was the blue of the ocean
and all of the rest that you could fit in a bill,
and all of the rest that you could fit in a bill.

Jack Harris

Streamer on a Kite

Listen to the sound of the swallow's lost song
harnessing the wind and saddling the unridden sun
the liver red fire at the heel of the sky
the beetle black wing of the swallow telling you, you can fly

Listen to the way that the longest branch groans
dripping worried sap and drying as the worried wind blows
all at once moves and all at once breathes
you and I bend as limber as two saplings

But I've had it in mind to tell you
I've seen you in the sky
you're the streamer on a kite

Listen to the sound of the endless back wheels
the galactic harvest hoard of the fecund silicon fields
the old dry well now safe under stone
the trembling earth, the pump of our hearts till we're gone

But I've had it in mind to tell you
I've seen you in the sky
you're the streamer on a kite

Iain Archer

The Last Song

Good Morning Janseungpo
waxen my wings
beads of the dawn
fall from golden strings.
I danced through a valley
of billowing sea
great shadows so noble
are far beneath.

And waves they were making
due west the direction
nets they were stretched out
and harm been done
so I tempered a song
though a song-bird she knows
her most beautiful notes
are the dying ones.

High in the slipstream
for miles I could see
dappled with scarlet
rippled in green
and dull painted metal
the hatches pulled up
snatch of a harpoon
and blood in the scrub.

And waves they were making
due west the direction
nets they were stretched out
and harm been done
so I tempered a song
though a song-bird she knows
her most beautiful notes
are the dying ones.

I feared to come closer
encircled the ship
taste made me uneasy
of shot in the air
the voices of engines
the turn of the screw
and screaming for bulls
at the rodeo.

And waves they were making
due west the direction
nets they were stretched out
and harm been done
so I tempered a song
though a song-bird she knows
her most beautiful notes
are the dying ones.

The catch in my chest
fell to the crests
with all living fibre
put fear to rest
and deep in the water
turning about
no more to the slaughter
will they be lead

Jess Morgan

an onnagata kami infests my forest

early morning
still wet from the night cool air
sunrise warming birds
singing like bird
like Charlie
on a wild one who I guess
actually was singing
like them
they accompany my cracked notes and
somehow overcherished words

so little time so much
to say and always
wondering to whom – perhaps
you. The
forest edges almost to my
door and the slip away
green fields
from the
hills other side to a
town
of chimneys and paper

beyond the endless sky
rises
like prayer smoke or the whipping
high white Himalayan
flags to some kind
of a
wonderful beyond

Jonathan Day

14

I don't want to be a white master

Yes, I'm white
but I don't want to be a white master.
I was born on the outskirts of Kiev,
in what we call the bandit region.
at three I learned what sex was,
at five - death,
at seven - fascism and violence,
at ten - poverty, labour and hunger.
At twenty I was accused of robbing the till at work
because it was me who needed the money most
but they lied. The general manager did it.
And at 21 the police named me as a thief
but they lied too. They did it.
"But you might be a murderer!" - they said as
I was kicked out of the dorm onto the street.
"She might rob or kill us!"
- said the husband of a friend who had invited me to stay.

Power has no charm or delight for me.
No regard, no solace for authority.

Yes, I'm white,
but I don't want to be a white master.
The white masters dehumanized me,
turned me into an object
that holds no potential of being a friend
or partner who feels worthy to be loved,
reduced me to being a safe way
to satisfy sexual desires,
a silent slave, serving personal,
and without consequence
invaded my personal space.
Once I was a believer.
then I became an atheist,
feminist, anarchist...

But suddenly
I froze with horror
because always
and everywhere
there is someone
who has decided
that he is better than any other.
This is the white master.
Alas,
there are many of us.

Eugene Comrade Cat Purpurovsky, translated by Paul Chilton

Midwinter Moon

This moon is far–fetched:
the thinnest of crescents frosted
into a deep sky.
                    It's perfect
as a story: I expect shepherds
and starlight as a minimum,

though I don't need them
to announce themselves
as miracles.
                    It's enough
to go out in it, hear the crunch
and give of frozen ground
underfoot, stretch my arms up
through the bare trees
open my mouth
                    to receive
the season's sacrament:
the first flakes of snow on my tongue

Liz Lefroy

Behind The Glass

I could see the half moon away behind the window
I could see the half me so close behind the glass
sometime in the night like a bell rings through the quiet
sometime in the night I could hold the second's pass
and I could hear

In the stillness of the night I was drawn across the doorway
in the dark glancing of the night I was held upon a road
and though I never knew why we'll bend ourselves to waiting
in the inking of the night, then we knew the seconds slowed
and we could listen

If they can hang the rain from the tallest tower
they'll never find the way when the light goes out
and if we can break the chain at the clearest hour
which of you could really stay here behind the glass?

Robin Beatty

沿途有妳陪行

沿途遇知音給我輕送樂韻
寒夜冷風吹不進入我心
皆因有妳陪行
芳踪與小提琴
深深感恩
這我一直想擁有

煩悶之思緒不復再
人情是與非我對這沒好感
溫馨看浮雲
音詩耳在聞
飄忽於空間
今天身心己樂透

原來夢與真似是沒解究
呆坐這一刻想愴我的心
痴痴想想如何
懶得理會旁人
獨自遊魂
享受只得我獨有

Edmond Lam

Pretending to sleep

I chose to waste our last few moments
together
not telling you I needed you
or asking why you cried

As you leant over and kissed our foreheads
for the very last time
I rolled over and turned my back on you
and pretended to sleep
pretended to sleep
pretended to sleep

and I remember the last words you spoke
over your shoulder as you left the room
you said
look after your mother boys
look after your mother boys
look after your mother boys

another excuse for a day off school
another reason to move away
another veil, another shroud
another day, another cloud

Now I'm a father and a husband too
and I don't fear you no more
Instead of looking up to you
Feel I'm standing by your side
standing by your side
standing by your side

another excuse for a day off school
another reason to move away
another veil, another shroud
another day, another cloud

Did not wait your turn
Did not take your place in line

You jumped the queue
fell right through
did not feel the love

Rob Dunsford

Ma Chérie

Ma Chérie, tes yeux,
sont aussi bleus que le ciel
tes lèvres, comme le miel
et ta voix, je dirais, ma foi
est comme un oiseau
Ton visage est si beau

Ma chérie, ma chérie
ma chérie, ma chérie

Ton nez, comme celui d'une fée
ton sourire qui me fait tellement rire
tes oreilles, même plus belles que ton nez
tes cheveux, qui me rend tellement heureux

Ma chérie, ma chérie
ma chérie, ma chérie

Fergus Reid

Andrew Kulman

Mob Ray

organ donor with a loaded truck
around town hound for his lady luck
surf rock drummer with a heavy load
rockabilly screams on a dead end road
scrap iron bands in suburban wood
puking out songs like Zahn said we should
wake up drunk playing in the hall
abalone yearning and a barn yard brawl

Brad Fernholz

Journeyman Miller

I've changed my mind but don't worry, I'll probably change it again

Take a look at me brother/sister, it's always a rainy day

I'm a journeyman miller, always a rolling on/ever a rolling stone

There's a fisherman's daughter, she is the one I know/love

One too many tears that I didn't cry, one too many tears

What if they could bring, healing to your door

One too many days that I just do, one too many days

Walking in my sleep, not finding anything new

Nathan Tromans

Andrew Kulman

Arms of Clare

Dancing 'round in summer skies
clothed in leaves of green
They never saw his shaded heart
it wasn't what it seemed
And each night he would let down his hair
each night he would dream of being
in the arms of Clare

Some believed his illness true
was bought on by a demons lie
Wide eyed now he tried to drink
all the wine he'd been denied
And each night he would let down his hair
each night he would long to be
in the arms of Clare

Waiting for the storm to clear
and hoping for it soon
He hid inside an empty well
and watched the growing moon
And each night he would let down his hair
each night how he wished he was
in the arms of Clare

In a Scottish town he told his tale
and made his mother cry
Loved ones and friends never understood
and slowly watched him die
And each night somewhere out there
and each night he's found his comfort
deep in the arms of Clare

Dan Donovan

Around the World

I can't believe what I've just learned
my inner feelings are all starting now to burn
and I'm less and less concerned
we're hoping all around the world

My crying people it's your turn
my crying people we've a freedom to be earned
we've been working on it forever
all around the world

And if you know what you've got to give
you've got to give it all
the future's in our hands so don 't you dare play small
join the Movement all around the world

You took me to your Mother's house
you put the sweetest Turkish honey in my mouth
we all love to kiss and hug
all around the world

Meet me by the stream
I've been living in a dream
and all our people have been too
wanting to get next to you

I want to be your lover
and never love another
and it comes right to you right now singing from the start
And everybody feels it beating in their hearts
it comes to you love more and more each day
and you will hear her singing on your dying day

Luke Concannon

There's no such thing as the happy ever after

There's no such thing as happiness, won't waste my life just looking for you.
Bury my head in a bottle,
don't want to wake up just get out of my brains now.

I've wasted all my time, just looking for.
someone to be my one.
but now I know that it's me,
that I don't need someone else to be free.

So I'll say it again that I know in the end.

There's no such thing as happiness,
just someone'll make the nights grow warmer.
take my hand and make me cry,
but always remember that you can't rely on.

And I wasted all this time, just hoping for,
someone to be my one
but now I know that it's true,
in spite of you, that I can fight by myself.
And if only I knew you believed in it too,
yes you.
Now I don't need, someone else to be free.

So I'll say it again that I know in the end.

There's no such thing, no
there's no such thing

Kev Adams

Bullet in the baby

The heart beats, regular as gunfire
in the stillness the whole mouth twists
the eyes narrow, knuckle-white
and cling. Outside
there are arms full of bodies
hills full of tired armies.

'Embrace me now, sweet mother
I am here in spite of death
fickle winds or sudden men.
Neither winter time nor war contained me
I am the Holy Fist
an embryonic saint and sacrifice
the final price
whose moment dulls the bullet's edge
to drive a wedge between the cradle and...'

A thin scream splits the skull
a dog barks, men run
in the stillness, the whole mouth twists

the face speaks for the landscape.

Phil Thomson

Potato Flower

If we listen to Potato Flower,
thrown purple on the hill,
we may understand the state of man,
bowed to a lover's will,
if we listen to their peaty mouths
all mingles in the meal,
and the song therein their tubered voices
peeling –

How low, how small, how base are we
to flower here, most gloriously

If we listen to the plumy stones,
dropped damson on the dun,
as they sing in balmy evening,
up t'wards a bloody sun,
if we understand the game,
the measure and the rule,
and how the outcome fits the teacher to the
schooling

How low, how small, how base are we
to flower here, most gloriously

If we clamour for the breathy tones,
breathed outwards of a gable,
and how the lovers pass their confidences
'cross a burning table,
if we circumscribe the mottled mauves
tongued tender to the throat,
we may glean the song that sings inside the
doting

How low, how small, how base are we
to flower here, most gloriously

Jack Harris

Outlets

In a world made of power outlets
reach out to touch
electric shock
chronic electric trauma
I can't even count the burns
again and again
some people have nowhere to hide
from their own vulnerability
and the only shelter
is denial
Nothing hurts
Nothing happened
I don't exist at all
let's make the world safe
let's make the world safe for all

Eugene Comrade Cat Purpurovsky, translated by Paul Chilton

juniper may leave
on a summer's day
wooden ships
slide around a
brown river's bend to a
turreted town full of
sound, alive
with dandelion
seeds

stay child for
a while
stay child

juniper may leave
on an
autumn's day
leaves flying
wild their
muddy yellow remembers the sun
yellow haired
corn has
come and gone

juniper may leave
on a
winter's day
Wenceslas white
all is quiet sleeping as
good as dead the
ice's blue knife
gnaws knuckles frost fingers your
heart but
the black mountain
stands
on the summit the
white gate is wide

juniper may leave
on a
spring day
awakening with the leaves a
zephyr troubles her
hair the
bright painted flowers are
unaware of
her laughter
clear that
fills the air until
it fades
like all things a
passing shadow on a
forest road

Jonathan Day

Annie of Greyfriars.

Now that I've found you
don't tell me go
don't send me out dear in the cold
holes in my boots and foot rot
I mean no harm.

Cuts on your fingers
elbows in brine
wind beating down your gutting line
I'll help you wash the salt off.
I mean no harm.

Annie of Greyfriars
works on the yard
just stuck a fish-Knife through my heart
I have been rough and tumbled
I mean no harm.

When dark clouds come rushing over
and thunder is rolling on
she flashes a look like lightening for me but
one day they may see calm
in her hard weathered palm
she has my heart.

Now that I'm near you
don't back away
wind burned the proud look on your face
walk with me on the South Quay
I mean no harm.

Harder than working
harder than steel
look at me walking on your wheel
fish me out of the barrel
I mean no harm.

When dark clouds come rushing over
and thunder is rolling on
she flashes a look like lightening for me but
one day they may see calm
in her hard weathered palm
she has my heart.

Annie of Greyfriars
works in the yard.

Jess Morgan

Andrew Kulman

Black Mountain Quarry

With the pallor of a spook
and the wiry gait I undertook
there hung from fraying thread
my heart inside my hopeful chest
the gravel underfoot
the slow incline that bends my boot
I have lost my precious will
I have burned what I set out to fulfil

But I could dig a fresh gem from the black mountain quarry
oh my heart is stone cold and my soul is full of worry
but I'll be waiting for the thaw like a little bird told me
oh Black Mountain Quarry

The rooks cry with remiss
as if to say 'I'm tired of this'
while on their sable wing
the stars, the moon and everything
that emanates a glow
is consumed and never spoken of
I too would meet this fate
for no glow have I recovered yet

But I could dig a fresh gem from the black mountain quarry
oh my heart is stone cold and my soul is full of worry
but I'll be waiting for the thaw like a little bird told me
oh Black Mountain Quarry

Iain Archer

Body and Blood

Division God's mission of our saving race
a salvation station chock full of grace
divine wine pouring from the stone's face
drive a wedge with the sledge so to take the place
Body Blood Machine leaving little space

Daring hearts seem mean
but do we know the love they really mean
the Body Blood Machine
puts faith up in the place of you and me.

Race killing face on the river bank
scribes prophesy a think tank
fear stabled table stealing for the bank blood drawn borders of the mandate
faith's shaming power the forward flank.

Staring at the Body Blood machine
thinking that you know what it means
staring at the Body Blood Machine
that doesn't want us to know what it means
bass beat to death by the country fear.
Sacred cows marching to be rendered deer.
Raving likes ratings like we always do
voters clicking levers dumping stock in you
markets holy order will come save you too.

The Body and Blood Machine
doesn't want us to know what it means
the Body Blood Machine
puts fear up in the place of all our dreams.

Brad Fernholz

All We've Ever Known

Raised beneath a tin roof
me and my sister cut the peat slabs for the fire
and we'd count the stars on the way back home
that was all we'd ever known

Dad he kept his fiddle by the bar stool
climbed the Reek, to see the Lady's face
and he'd count the stars on the way back home
it was all he'd ever known

He said we'll rise with the cold water
stay awake til the last
we're going to hear all the noise
and sing with the great voice

Winters drew like the face in the corvid mirror
and the rain came ratting at the tin door
some said the ground will fall and strip us all to bone
but it was all we'd ever known

The old ways conveyed us, arcing from the valley
like the seeds before the cutting winds are blown
walked through the nights, before the rising sun
from all we'd ever known

He said we'll rise with the cold water
stay awake til the last
we're going to hear all the noise
and sing with the great voice

We wound our way to the waves of a wide shoreline
and the edge of the land we called our own
the boat man called as the last light left an outline
of all we've ever known

With the dawn we woke to the sight of a strange horizon
almighty spires and towers replaced the sky
blanked out the stars, and the way back home
and all we've ever known

Robin Beatty

I Dance Alone, Thursday, 15 May 2014

I didn't feel at ease until I leant to dance alone.

There was nothing to learn, except
to understand the need to push back the table,
to dress for the dance as if dressing for a lover,
to choose music which moves with itself.

There was nothing to learn, but that
the moment I kick off my shoes,
the moment I turn down the lights,
the moment I dance for myself,
is the moment I feel free.

Liz Lefroy

Andrew Kulman.

Millionaire

If you're counting the scars on his knees
he's a millionaire
If you're counting missed opportunities
he's a millionaire

Nothing in my pockets - just holes and bits of fluff
I never felt so weighed down - by all this useless stuff

If you're counting tears and heartbeats
I'm a millionaire
If you're counting fears and goosebumps
I'm a millionaire

If you're counting her blisters and bruises
she's a millionaire
If you're counting beggars and choosers
she's a millionaire

Nothing in my pockets - just holes and bits of fluff
I never felt so weighed down - by all this useless stuff
Nothing in my pockets - just holes and bits of fluff
I never felt so weighed down - by all this useless stuff

Rob Dunsford

Last time

Cannot disguise this, wrestle my feelings, harder just knowing, still I'm not sure if trouble just speaking, when words are misleading, these thorns in my pocket, presence unwanted

Last time, last time we could be right here, right here you and me, you know, you know it's time to let go

Start hearing voices, they're moving around us, blasting the borders, coming alive with
Looking for answers lead on to discover, we know we don't know why, this is beginning

Last time, last time we could be right here, right here you and me, you know, you know it's time to let go

Paul Archer

The Ballad of Edith Swan-neck and King Harold

Her name is Edith
she moves like a swan across the field
of fallen soldiers
It's getting late now
the light is swiftly fading behind the woods
the sun is blood red

She wears a white dress
her contour carves an S shape against the sky
Her face is lowered
she moves amongst them
the dying the dismembered and the maimed
But she can't find him

Still she sifts through the field
turning over faces here and there
she lightly touches a young man's hair
like a pony muzzles thistles in the snow

A squire approaches
his horse all gleaming sweat upon the flank
He bows deeply
they think they've found it
a body with an arrow through the head
But they can't be certain

So she walks over
his features are too broken to really know
she lifts his armour
and there she knows him
A body she's caressed oft times before
her one true lover
her one true lover
Her one true lover

Fergus Reid

53

Symphony for a Broken Piano (Will I Ever See You Again.)

A broken piano rots discarded, yellow keys that hold no tune,
I romance a shimmering memory and on this silver night it's you,
the blind beggar shakes his tin to the rhythm of the rain,
and he sees much more than me, will I ever, will I ever, see you again.

Out on this black highway, the diamond crows and I,
I need you like water in a dry and desperate time,
the lament and lull of ivory could ease these arms of pain,
and the questioning of the winds.
Will I ever, will I ever, see you again,

How I long for a melody, to make this burden light,
for a tiny candle burning in the long and endless night,
as time plays its endless waltz, with a lost and sad refrain,
the boneman lifts my old piano, gone forever,
gone forever in the rain.

His horse will pull it's rusted frame, we'll never hear it play again,
the songs that echoed off these walls,
leaving empty rooms and halls,
as it jangles it's last song down the lane.
Will I ever, will I ever, see you again.

Gavin Monaghan

A Song is Like a Lover

A song is like a lover, that you so long to know
all her holy secrets, (she won't ever show)
a tender for her loving, gamble for her eye
all in all we stand alone, (defeated by her charm)

I undertake to always make, love like I am dying
I undertake to always make (love like I am dying)

A kind o' misadventure, cruel and tender smile
sadness in a twilight hour, you break a broken heart
oh Lord of the abandoned, a song I'd love to sing
for all the bitter sweetness, a humble song can bring

I undertake to always make, love like I am dying
I undertake to always make (love like I am dying)

Nathan Tromans

Living on dreams

Ragged clothing and ragged hair, don't need no bedding, sleep anywhere,
wherever you go you'll get there on time, you're leaving home with good dreams on
your mind.

And it's alright now, they'll make a fool of you somehow,
but it's alright when you're living on dreams.

Answers to questions take you high or low, some take forever, 'cos nobody knows.
Some tell you truly that it's mine all mine, but sundials in the moonlight always tell
the wrong time.

And it's alright now, they'll make a fool of you somehow,
but it's alright when you're living on dreams

I want you to tell me,
I just want to know,
do you have the power of love like that voice on the radio.

We got the power for light, power for food, power for warmth, we got the power to
move,
the hungry world would like a change of heart, 'cos it's living on dreams while the
light gets dark.

And it's alright now, they'll make a fool of you somehow,
and it's alright when you're living on dreams.

Kevin Dempsey

I want to be free

My thoughts are a blur
I can't remember why
and when my daughter sits next to me
she cries

She's a good one
looking after me well
a song or a kiss is heaven
getting stuck in this pain is hell

I wanna be free

Until my life runs out

I just want a cup of tea
why can't you understand me?
Oh bugger I can't say the words!

And when the Nurses move me
some times they shout and don't say please
I'm sorry I'm ill and causing you this trouble my love

I'm going in to this black hole
but I know I've got a soul

Luke Concannon

Jinx of Job

There's a black cat I'm singing to
with his ear down low
through the door he's leading me
which way, who knows?
A heavy sky blooms a fiery sun
and naked trees that cannot
run away, away from here
And at the end of each day
like some mystery play
the jinx of Job

Hunger lives inside this soul
and it will not die
the fruit is ripe and time has told
but you still deny
All this food before me now
just disappears away and how
how far, far from here
and at the end of each day
like some mystery play
the jinx of Job

Dan Donovan

Andrew Kulman   April

flower arranging

flower arranging
baby changing
body-building
sandwich filling
clown masking
never

hang-gliding
snowdrift sliding
flying kites
women's rights
life and soul
asking

window shopping
traffic hopping
money spinning
good beginnings
play acting
never

UFO sighting
pillow fighting
pleasing friends
bitter end
hide and seek
asking

plain sailing
always taking
always dreaming
hidden meanings
clown masking
never

high living
never giving
always time
TV rhymes
life or death
asking

Phil Thomson

Swollen River

My sweet night is dark, lights they are low,
a flicker, a blaze, a dance of light, rose up from your window

If I pitch a stone right at your pain, would you open the door again

My heart is a swollen river, yours girl is a deep dry well

Far from you in Ohio, where I was a curious man,
I sang my song a lonely while, to call my will and my way,
a shadow, a cloud, a vapour trail, return to your return

My heart is a swollen river, yours girl is a deep dry well

Nathan Tromans

That's where I belong

That's where I belong - in receipt of your whisper
gently in my ear, so only I can hear

That's where I belong
and it doesn't matter where you are
I need to be with you, you are my beating heart

There's a place where I go
right under your nose
that's where I'm strong
that's where I belong

That's where I belong - being listened to by you
hearing re-assurances
without providing cues

That's where I belong
that's where I want to stay
hearing that simple phrase -
repeated every day

There's a place where I go
right under your nose
that's where I'm strong
that's where I belong

Swimming through your generous words
you soothe my restless mind

Lying in a bed we built on promises
I know that I'll be fine

There's a place where I go
right under your nose
that's where I'm strong

Dan Whitehouse

Head High

Hold your head way up high
so high touches the sky
so high never look down
the futures bright so move on
the futures bright so move on

When you can't, can't find those pieces
the jigsaw in your mind
don't worry nothing is pure
no looking back it's onwards and on
no looking back it's onwards and on

You'll find a way to put things right
so right everything's fine
so fine floating along
you'll never look back no never look back
you'll never look back no never look back
Hold your head way up high
so high touches the sky
so high never look down
the futures bright so move on
the futures bright so move on

Ross Ainslie

Andrew Kulman

Sincerity

Love sick on a rainbow
dumb stuck in your window
fire in islands
life through my hands
let go of a jealous game
forcing fear to get some shame
take in and let it go
level myself and know

Tuned in the key we wrote
breath deep and clear my throat
it might be a travesty
or a moment of clarity

Sing of the joker too
spray paint and Elmer's glue
victims of circumstance
high cheeks and morbid stance
take in or be afraid
remember the things you said
careful the life you glean
speak what you really mean

Tuned in the key we wrote
breath deep and clear my throat
it might be a tragedy
or a moment of clarity
it could be a tragedy
but let's have sincerity

Moon shots in the morning
sailors take warning
acid rain inside my chest
snow cleanse and winters rest
ice water inside your veins
sharp tongue still remains
kill you with kindness
warm words to remind us

A tree in the forest
broke branches and little rest
a devil of detail
strong wind inside your sail
I'm sending my roots down
so spread word across the town
give me your best shot
that's all we've really got

Tuned in the key we wrote
breath deep and clear my throat
save me your charity
and your talk of simplicity
Tuned in the key we wrote
breath deep and clear my throat
it might be a tragedy
but I want sincerity
it might be a travesty
or a moment of clarity
but, let's have sincerity

Brad Fernholz

The Banks of Old Tahiti

The egrets and albatross
the lorikeets and gulls
fruit doves and hornbills
at the edges of the world
white sands, flashing seas
fish-hooks they make of pearl
cooking pots of yellow clay
on the banks of old Tahiti

From the sextant, we drew the charts
by night we read the skies
to a people, on an untold shore
beheld their lustrous eyes
and golden faces, fine to gaze upon
their legs were sleek and brown
these fair treasures, we exchanged
on the banks of old Tahiti

One more nail, one more nail
when the morning comes we'll fly the sail
when the morning comes we'll bid farewell
and turn to meet the weather
One more nail, one more nail
when the morning comes we'll face the gale
and yes we'll take what you have for sale
before we leave this world forever

The *Endeavor*, with her worthy load
was anchored off the shore
the people sought the iron things
they'd never seen before:
knives and rivets, iron rings,
fairleads, bolts and pins
exchanged to lie in tender arms
on the banks of old Tahiti

Half the galley, the cutlery
shackles and cleats
the troves of the ship's carpenter
all laid before their feet
in the dark the men crouched beneath the bilge
each prizing from the stem
the iron nails for one more night
on the banks of old Tahiti

One more nail, one more nail
when the morning comes we'll fly the sail
when the morning comes we'll bid farewell
and turn to meet the weather
One more nail, one more nail
when the morning comes we'll face the gale
and yes we'll take what you have for sale
before we leave this world forever

Robin Beatty

Dashboard Therapy

the road's so narrow and it seems so long
the river's so deep and the current's so strong
the ditches so deep and the hedges too high
through tarmac veins we course tonight

stop to wonder at the stars
weave our way through the isobars
chemical trails criss-cross the sky
but we never look road-kill in the eye

we survive on forecourt snacks
paying with cash just to cover our tracks
bottled water costs the same as fuel
but we buy it anyway 'cos it keeps us cool

we drive by night and sleep by day
driving all our cares away
tape cassettes and good company
our simple dashboard therapy

Rob Dunsford

Your war is denial

Burn truth like a candle
watch your ego dismantle
run free from the fighting
the truth is too frightening to say

When the start is the final
and your war is denial
you're making a new world
and words are the bullets today

but you could learn to fight it
if you'd only get united

Now where is the meaning
now reason is leaving
and you've got to hide it
but hiding is walking away

But you could learn to fight it
if you'd only get united

But you just keep walking away

Walking Walking Walking

Paul Archer

Andrew Kulman

Many Kettles

Out of my window
factories down below.
Cat on the roof top sleeps.
Rusty panels that leak.

I see the prison walls.
I see the market stalls.
I hear the tram-bells ring.
I smell the open drains.

What if just once at night
over these roofs took flight
fiery red Phoenix bird
sparks fly across the sky.

Factory can't be seen.
Prison cannot be seen.
Just like they hadn't been.
Just...

I know that this could be
For it is what I see.

Eugene Comrade Cat Purpurovsky, translated by Paul Chilton

Easter Morning

In Easter Morning's fledgling light,
with the lingering stars still burning,
I pulled myself into myself,
and thought about returning.

Though the manacles of night still held
the watchman at his station,
I thought of all I gave away,
and of my reputation.

On Easter Morning's changing face
was worn both hope and caution,
I couched myself in the common pain,
considering then my portion.

And I did confess some shade of doubt,
and begged of it some pardon,
but the mark of death was on the meal,
of Easter's waiting garden.

And I saw myself with fallen things,
with Lucifer and Laurel,
for I never meant to be the earth,
nor meant to be a quarrel.

But Fresh was all the sedge and rye,
the fragrant jasmine flowers,
and I thought of all that was to wake,
in these few waking hours.

In Easter Morning's fledgling light,
with the lingering stars still burning,
I pulled myself into myself,
and thought about returning,
I thought about returning,
I thought about returning.   *Jack Harris*

77

carved in bone naked
you stand
from a distant place and time – fire
in my hands
we shall be ashes, you
and I, who in these
moments burn from the
gun stab's sudden
fury or the quiet
pages turn
where have you come
from where will you go?
you're yellow like the corn
fields and white like the
snow

a strange bell ringing for
a clown bright dancing bird I
hope these flasks of ashes in the
snow will
feel the sun's return the
millions before us (on this
star splashed midnight sky) our
silent
dusty passion gives meaning to
their lives

a red haired widow's voiceless
crying a
cigarette's incense circling slowly
toward the sky a war dead
babies innocent eyes tell
us to live like
fire If
they could speak the
thousands crucified I
believe they'd speak of

love and sun and sky with
laughter
in their eyes

where have you come from where
will you go? you're
yellow
like the corn fields and white like the
snow you're
brown
like the earth and blue
like the sky I
will live forever in
the half light of
your eyes

Jonathan Day

Modern World

A loose end and a hot day
what a match made up there, I'd say
for pulling on your work jeans
and throwing a cigarette in the yard.
We can always make like springtime
with new paint over old
'til the chain snaps clean off our machine
and they don't make them any more

Surely a blessing you are
and I'll only spoil your fun
see me I'm an old soul
I don't think I belong in your modern world

You could always see the good things
and I'd make do to make your heart sing
see the rust set in all over
as being only surface deep
yet I'd give you racing handles
and strip you back for speed
treat you kind and paint you claret
if you make it home with me

surely a blessing you are
and I'll only spoil your fun
see me I'm an old soul
I don't think I belong in your modern world

I remember you best in June.
You took it oh so well
changed clothes and your tune
down in the dunes
out by California Sands
and you're red around the eyes now
but have it on the chin
you're looking bonnie with the wind
in them salt water curls

surely a blessing you are
and I'll only spoil your fun
me I'm an old soul
I don't think I belong in your modern world

Jess Morgan

Contributors

Kev Adams is a guitarist and songwriter most known for his work with **Dexy's Midnight Runners,** including co-authoring their classic *Come On Eileen.*

Ross Ainslie's solo albums have been nominated for **Album of the Year** at the Scots Trad Music Awards and made the top 10 of the **Sunday Herald's Top 50** Scottish Album. He collaborates widely – with **Treacherous Orchestra** who made the **2015 Album of the Year** Award Nominations, with Dougie Maclean, Salsa Celtica, Jarlath Henderson and Mairearad Green.

Iain Archer has made a number of solo records and collaborates widely. He won an Ivor Novello award for his work with **Snow Patrol** (#1 chart hit **Run**), was nominated for another for his work with **Jake Bugg** and received a Grammy Award nomination this year for *Hold Back the River* which he co-wrote with **James Bay**. He is part of **Tired Pony** with Peter Buck, Miriam Kaufmann and Gary Lightbody and is Visiting Professor at Leeds College of Music.

Paul Archer is singer, songwriter and guitarist with **Burning Codes** who perform widely, were recently featured on **Sky Arts** and provided some of the music for CBS Television's *Aquaman.*

Robin Beatty is guitarist songwriter and singer with **The Fair Rain,** formerly **The Old Dance School.** The band were part of **Songlines Top Of The World,** and won **The Scotsman's Album of the Year.**

Luke Concannon works solo and as part of chart topping band **Nizlopi.**

Jonathan Day is a critically acclaimed musician, writer and image maker who performs and exhibits internationally. He also runs BirTh, the Transmedia Research Hub and has edited and illustrated this collection.

Kevin Dempsey is a seminal guitarist and singer, whose influence has been felt most keenly in the folk world, where he has performed with **Dando Shaft, Whippersnapper, Dave Swarbrick, Joe Broughton** and currently with **Rosie Carson**. He has also played with **Alice Coltrane, Percy Sledge** and motown band **The Marvelettes.**

Dan Donovan has serially inspired a hugely dedicated following though his incarnations as **The Tribe of Dan**, solo work and currently with **King Kool.**

Rob Dunsford is a songwriter from the Welsh borders who has featured on a tribute to master writer **Townes Van Zant** and contributed to classic Shropshire Hill Country song collections.

Eugene Comrade Cat Purpurovsky is the musical producer, lyricist, hurdy-gurdy player and vocalist of **tAngerinecAt**. The lyrics are translated by **Paul Chilton.**

Brad Fernholz lives and writes in rural Minnesota. He is a founding contributor to **Duluth's Homegrown** festival. His new album *Crow Moon,* with his band **Man On The Moon**, is soon to be released.

Jack Harris was a **South by South-West** showcasing artist at 17. He was also the youngest, as well as the only non-American person ever to win the New Folk song writing award at the **Kerrville Folk Festival, Texas.** He has toured with **Cara Dillon** and **Dick Gaughan**. His work was included in **The Telegraph 10 Roots**/Folk albums of 2012.

Ed Lam is a musician and photographer working in **Macau**. He writes in Chinese and English and speaks Guangdong Hwa.

Liz Lefroy has published a number of books of poetry and performed widely, including with Poet Laureate **Carol Ann Duffy** and Welsh National Poet **Gillian Clarke**. Her words have been set to music on a number of occasions.

Gavin Monaghan is a sought after writer and producer, whose encyclopaedic credits include **The Jesus and Mary Chain, The Editors, Robert**

Plant, Scott Matthews and many more.

Jess Morgan has toured extensively in Europe and the US and has collaborated widely, notably with **Hans Petter Gundersen** and the **Paper Aeroplanes.**

Fergus Reid writes in English and French, often taking inspiration from his Shropshire home.

Phil Thomson is a lyricist and visual artist with a particular interest in Christian music. He has written for **Cliff Richard** and composed a number of popular contemporary hymns. His works here are for **Adrian Snell** and progressive rock band **Gentle Giant.**

Nathan Tromans is a photographer and musician with a particular interest in family history and his home landscape. He performed at this year's **Shifting Worlds** event alongside **Faye Claridge, Jeremy Deller, David Nash** and **Martin Parr.**

Dan Whitehouse is a songwriter of great emotional intelligence who has recently toured with **Eddi Reader, Kris Drever** and **Lau.**